GOD RESTORES THE BROKEN

How Faithful, God-Centered Habits Lead
to Lasting Transformation and Renewal

TANIA SANDHU

Copyright © 2025 by Tania Sandhu

All rights reserved.

No part of this book may be reproduced, distributed, or transmitted in any form without prior written permission.

Published by Tania Sandhu

ISBN: 979-8-9925259-0-8

This publication is designed to provide accurate and authoritative information in regard to the subject matter covered. It is sold with the understanding that neither the author nor the publisher is engaged in rendering legal, investment, accounting or other professional services. While the publisher and author have used their best efforts in preparing this book, they make no representations or warranties with respect to the accuracy or completeness of the contents of this book and specifically disclaim any implied warranties of merchantability or fitness for a particular purpose. No warranty may be created or extended by sales representatives or written sales materials. The advice and strategies contained herein may not be suitable for your situation. You should consult with a professional when appropriate. Neither the publisher nor the author shall be liable for any loss of profit or any other commercial damages, including but not limited to special, incidental, consequential, personal, or other damages.

To my two boys, who inspire me every day.

And for those seeking more—
May this journey bring you closer to God.

TABLE OF CONTENTS

THE MEANING BEHIND THE COVER 1

EMBRACING GOD'S TRANSFORMATIVE PLAN 3

FROM BROKENNESS TO BREAKTHROUGH 7

SURRENDERING TO GOD 17

EMBRACING A GROWTH MINDSET 29

BUILDING CONSISTENT HABITS 39

THE POWER OF VISUALIZATION 51

THE POWER OF GRATITUDE 63

THE POWER OF FORGIVENESS 75

THE POWER OF PRAYER 89

THE POWER OF AFFIRMATIONS 101

EMBRACING THE FUTURE 115

CLOSING REFLECTION 125

CELEBRATING GOD'S FAITHFULNESS 133

SCRIPTURE GUIDE 139

THANK YOU FOR READING 163

THE MEANING BEHIND THE COVER

A SYMBOL OF RESTORATION

The bowl on the cover represents Kintsugi, the ancient Japanese art of repairing broken pottery with gold. Rather than discarding shattered pieces, Kintsugi embraces the cracks, highlighting them with gold to create something even stronger and more beautiful than before.

This mirrors the heart of God Restores the Broken. Just as a Kintsugi artist restores broken pottery, God restores our lives—taking our pain, trauma, loss, and doubt and mending them with His grace, love, and truth. Our scars are not signs of weakness; they are proof of His healing power, reminders that what was once broken can be made whole again.

Through faith, surrender, and renewal, God doesn't just fix our brokenness—He transforms it, making us more resilient, radiant, and purpose-filled than before. Just as Kintsugi turns brokenness into beauty, God restores us, strengthening us with His love and wisdom.

INTRODUCTION

EMBRACING GOD'S TRANSFORMATIVE PLAN

Life moves through seasons of joy and heartbreak, each shaping us in unexpected ways. I've been through those dark, uncertain moments when it felt impossible to believe that God was still at work. Yet, I've learned that it's often in our brokenness that His most transformative work begins.

This book is my story, and it's an invitation for you to lean into God's love, trust His perfect plan, and embrace the transformation He offers. It's not about blame or regrets—it's about discovering the power of God's healing grace. Through my journey, I've seen how He can take the shattered pieces of our lives and craft something beautiful. If you're facing heartbreak, disappointment, or unmet expectations, I want to remind you of this truth: God's love is steadfast, His promises are sure, and His plans for you are good.

Have you ever wondered how God could use the broken pieces of your life to create something beautiful? I certainly have. I doubted, I cried, and I wondered if God was even listening. But in those moments, His Word became my anchor, His peace became my refuge, and His strength carried me forward. Surrendering to Him revealed a deeper sense of identity—one rooted not in my circumstances, but in Christ.

Jeremiah 29:11 (NIV) reminds us of God's heart for His people: ***"For I know the plans I have for you," declares the Lord, "plans to prosper you and not to harm you, plans to give you hope and a future."*** This promise became a lifeline for me during my journey. Even when life felt unbearable, I clung to the assurance that God's purpose remained unshaken.

God's work in my life wasn't just about mending what was broken; it was about making me whole. He took my pain and began transforming it into a reflection of His glory. That process required trust, patience, and a willingness to let go of my own plans in exchange for His. It wasn't easy—I stumbled; I resisted—but each step brought me closer to Him.

Throughout these pages, I'll share the scriptures that sustained me, the moments that tested me, and the tools that helped me rebuild. You'll find journal prompts to help you reflect and engage with God's work in your life. My prayer is that this book doesn't just offer encouragement but that it becomes a companion in your own journey of transformation. I hope it helps you experience God's unshakable love and uncover the beauty He's creating in your life.

Life, as we know, is unpredictable. It's full of twists, heartbreaks, and challenges that stretch our faith. I've come to see that in every mess, there is a message; in every trial, a testimony; and in every broken story, an opportunity for God to write a new ending. This book is an invitation to step into that new story—to let God take the pen and craft a narrative of hope, healing, and transformation.

No matter where you are on your journey—whether you are struggling to hold on or beginning to see the light—know this: God is with you. He sees your pain, hears your prayers, and works all things together for good (Romans 8:28, NIV). He is the ultimate healer, restorer, and redeemer, and He desires to bring beauty from the ashes of your life.

As you turn these pages, I pray that you will see God's hand in your story, just as I've seen Him in mine. May you feel His gentle guidance, His refining love, and His unwavering presence. Your story is not over. With God, it is only just beginning.

CHAPTER ONE

FROM BROKENNESS TO BREAKTHROUGH

SHATTERED DREAMS

I never imagined my life would fall apart in this way. Sitting alone in the silence of my despair, I faced the painful truth: my marriage was over. Twelve years of my life—my hopes, my dreams, and the foundation I had built my world upon—crumbled in an instant.

"God, what just happened? Why weren't my prayers answered?"

In that raw moment, I found myself questioning everything. I wondered, *why am I the only one fighting for us?* The constant feeling of being unloved, overlooked, and abandoned—each one a dagger to my soul—slowly drained my sense of worth. I doubted myself. I wondered if somehow, I had failed. But the pain went deeper than just the end of my marriage. It was the unseen scars of emotional abuse, the silent wounds that linger long after the words are spoken.

Emotional abuse is insidious—it doesn't leave physical marks, but it distorts your reality, making you feel small, unworthy of love. For someone who believed wholeheartedly in God's unconditional love, it was nearly impossible to reconcile His promises with the constant rejection I faced.

"The Lord is near to the brokenhearted and saves the crushed in spirit." (Psalm 34:18, NIV)

But in that moment, I couldn't feel His presence.

WRESTLING WITH MY REALITY

Our marriage had never been perfect. From the start, it was a struggle. The promises we made during premarital counseling seemed like distant, beautiful words, but hollow when faced with the reality of unmet expectations, disappointments, and slowly eroding trust. While I wasn't without fault, I was the one who kept hoping, the one who fought for us, even when the battle felt impossible.

As a born-again Christian, I wrestled with my faith. *How could I feel undeserving of love, so broken in my marriage, yet still believe in God's love for me?* Years of emotional neglect had worn me down, and I no longer knew how to reconcile the truth of God's love with my reality. The pain of emotional abuse shattered my soul piece by piece, convincing me I was unworthy, unlovable, and hopeless.

For a Christian, this struggle is a double-edged sword. Our worth is meant to be anchored in Christ, not our circumstances. But when your reality tells a different story, it's hard to hold on. I was told time and again, *"Your worth is in Christ, not in your marriage."* I knew these words to be true in my mind, but my heart—shattered by pain—couldn't catch up.

On top of it all, I battled depression and anxiety—silent companions that deepened my isolation. The emotional weight was suffocating, and I felt completely lost.

WRESTLING WITH GOD

When I uncovered the truth—the lies and deceit—it hit me hard. But I still had children to care for. *How would they cope with the divorce? How would they adjust, especially with their own special needs and the demands for stability and routine?* I carried that weight on my shoulders alone, and it was crushing.

I pleaded with God. *"Please, God, don't let it end this way."*

But my prayers seemed unanswered. My then-husband moved out that summer, and soon after, the divorce papers were filed. That was the darkest season of my life. I cried endlessly, consumed by grief, as the life I had envisioned slipped away before my eyes.

Yet, in my deepest despair, I turned to God as never before. I dove into His Word, spent hours praying, and surrendered everything to Him. My prayer became simple, earnest: *God, if it's Your will, rebuild this marriage.*

"Call to me and I will answer you and tell you great and unsearchable things you do not know." (Jeremiah 33:3, NIV)

SURRENDER AND RENEWAL

To my surprise, my then-husband and I began talking again. In a moment of hope against all logic, I asked him to give us another chance. Emotional abuse clouds your judgment. It keeps you clinging to hope even when there's no evidence to support it. I believed in God's power to transform, in the possibility of a miracle. I prayed for a "God at work" story—a restoration of our marriage that would glorify Him.

My then-husband agreed. We began what I thought was reconciliation, but the truth soon became evident: there was no remorse for the betrayal, no apology, no real effort toward healing. Still, I leaned into God. I held fast to my faith, even when the path forward seemed unclear.

MEETING GOD ON THE BRIDGE

During this season, I embarked on a journey of self-care—something I had long neglected. I began walking every day, listening to audiobooks on personal growth, building better habits, and discovering God's unrelenting love. And it was during these walks that I met God in ways I never expected.

There was one place—a bridge—that became my sacred space. As reconciliation faltered, I realized I needed to focus on my own healing. I visited the bridge daily, pausing to pray, process, and listen for God's voice. In that quiet place, God began to rebuild me. I learned gratitude, forgiveness, perseverance, and—most powerfully—my true identity in Christ. Slowly, God was transforming me from the inside out, showing me that my worth wasn't defined by my marriage but by Him.

"But those who hope in the Lord will renew their strength. They will soar on wings like eagles; they will run and not grow weary, they will walk and not be faint." (Isaiah 40:31, NIV)

A TURNING POINT

Nearly a year after our reconciliation, the truth came crashing down again: the betrayal had never ceased. But this time, I was no longer the same. Through my prayers and surrender, God had rebuilt my strength piece by piece. His work in me allowed clarity to replace confusion and courage to overcome fear. With unwavering confidence, I chose to end the marriage—this time, on my terms, empowered by the strength He had given me.

I clung to Proverbs 3:5-6: ***"Trust in the Lord with all your heart and lean not on your own understanding; in all your ways submit to Him, and He will make your paths straight."*** This verse now held a depth of meaning I could never have imagined before.

GOD'S PLAN, NOT MINE

The divorce process was painful and gut-wrenching. But even in the agony, God carried me. I held tightly to my daily routines—devotionals, prayer, forgiveness, affirmations, walks, and time spent on that bridge with

God. These rituals grounded me, even when the pull of despair threatened to overwhelm me.

Looking back, I see now that God was always at work. His answers to my prayers weren't what I expected, but they were what I needed. He didn't fix my husband or my marriage—He fixed me.

REFLECTION QUESTIONS

As we begin this journey together, take a moment to reflect on your own story.

What are the areas in your life where you've felt broken or abandoned?

How can you invite God into those spaces to begin His healing work?

REFLECTION VERSE

Take a moment to open your Bible and look up the verse provided below. Read it slowly and prayerfully, letting God speak to your heart through His Word. Once you've read it, take time to reflect on its meaning. Write down how it applies to your journey, what it teaches you about God, or how it encourages your faith. Let this be an opportunity to deepen your connection with Him through His Word.

Verse: *Psalm 126:5*

Reflection: As you read this verse, consider how God can use even your deepest pain to create joy and transformation. What does this promise say about God's ability to redeem your circumstances?

JOURNAL PROMPT/PRAYER

Journal Prompt:

What scripture has spoken to you in moments of brokenness?

How can you let God's Word guide you today?

Prayer: Lord, my heart is heavy, and I feel lost. Help me find Your strength in Your Word. Speak to me through Your promises and remind me that You are near. Amen.

CHAPTER TWO

SURRENDERING TO GOD

THE STRUGGLE TO SURRENDER

Surrendering to God is one of the hardest steps in our spiritual journey. It requires vulnerability and a willingness to let go of control, especially when life feels overwhelming. For me, this struggle was deeply personal. Pain and confusion clouded my heart, and the thought of releasing control seemed impossible. *How could I let go when the future was so uncertain? How could I surrender when everything in me wanted to fight for what I believed should happen?*

As humans, we are wired to want control. It's how we navigate life's challenges and uncertainties. I clung tightly to the idea that if I worked harder, prayed longer, or tried more, I could fix everything—my marriage, my emotions, and my family's future. But the harder I tried, the more exhausted and disillusioned I became. My strength was limited. My understanding was flawed. I was fighting a losing battle.

It's in moments like these that God meets us. He doesn't expect us to have it all figured out or to bring perfection to the table. He simply asks us to trust Him. Proverbs 3:5-6 (NIV) became my lifeline: *"Trust in the Lord with all your heart and lean not on your own understanding; in all your ways submit to Him, and He will make your paths straight."* Surrendering to God doesn't mean giving up; it means giving in to His better plan. It's acknowledging that His ways are higher, and His understanding far surpasses our own.

THE IMPORTANCE OF SURRENDER

Surrendering to God is not a sign of weakness but of profound faith. It's an act of submission that says, "Lord, I trust You with everything." James 4:7 (NIV) reminds us, ***"Submit yourselves, then, to God. Resist the devil, and he will flee from you."*** Submission to God is not passive; it's an active, intentional choice to trust Him over the fears and lies that pull us away from His presence.

I remember a time when I was so consumed with trying to control my circumstances that I couldn't see beyond my exhaustion. The moment I finally let go and whispered, *"Lord, I can't do this alone,"* I felt an overwhelming sense of peace settle over me. It felt as though a weight had been lifted off my chest, and for the first time, I could breathe deeply. As 1 Peter 5:7 (NIV) says, ***"Cast all your anxiety on Him because He cares for you."***

Surrender also opens our hearts to experience God's love more fully. It's a declaration that His grace is enough, that His love is constant and unchanging. We don't have to earn it; we simply need to receive it. Surrender allows us to rest in His grace and trust that His plans are far better than anything we could imagine for ourselves.

THE SCIENCE OF LETTING GO

From a psychological perspective, surrendering control is a counterintuitive yet transformative practice. The brain craves certainty and predictability, which is why letting go can feel so unnatural. The amygdala, the part of the brain responsible for processing fear and stress, often activates when we face uncertainty, prompting us to cling tightly to what we can control. Yet, research shows that practices like prayer, meditation, and mindfulness—activities that focus on releasing control—help reduce the amygdala's activity and foster a sense of calm and trust.

Once we let go, we make room for God's guidance to transform not only our hearts but our entire way of living.

Dr. Caroline Leaf, a cognitive neuroscientist and Christian author, writes in *Switch On Your Brain* that focusing on God's promises and meditating on His Word can literally reshape our neural pathways. By replacing thoughts of fear and doubt with scripture and trust, we align our minds with His truth and experience peace. Philippians 4:6-7 (NIV) captures this beautifully:

"Do not be anxious about anything, but in every situation, by prayer and petition, with thanksgiving, present your requests to God. And the peace of God, which transcends all understanding, will guard your hearts and your minds in Christ Jesus."

LIVING A CHRIST-FILLED LIFE

Once we surrender, the next step is learning to live a Christ-filled life. This doesn't mean that life will become perfect or free of pain. But it does mean that we no longer face life's struggles alone. Christ is with us, guiding us, strengthening us, and offering us peace in the midst of our storms.

Living a Christ-filled life begins with daily commitment. It's the small, consistent choices that make a difference—waking up and praying before you start your day, turning to Scripture when overwhelmed, and seeking His presence in both joyous and painful moments. These habits, though simple, build a foundation of faith that sustains us through life's challenges.

Living a Christ-filled life isn't about striving for perfection but about leaning into God's strength. Each day presents an opportunity to grow closer to Him, to trust Him more deeply, and to reflect His love to those around us. When we center our lives on Christ, we find purpose and peace, even in the midst of uncertainty.

LESSONS FROM SCRIPTURE

The Bible is filled with examples of individuals who surrendered to God and saw His faithfulness unfold. Consider Mary, the mother of Jesus. When the angel told her she would bear the Son of God, she responded with complete trust: ***"I am the Lord's servant. May your word to me be fulfilled."*** (Luke 1:38, NIV) Her willingness to surrender, despite the risks and uncertainties, shows the power of trusting God's plan.

Similarly, Abraham's faith in God was tested when he was asked to sacrifice his son Isaac. Abraham's willingness to surrender his most precious gift demonstrated his trust in God's promises. In the end, God provided a ram in place of Isaac, proving that His plans are always good (Genesis 22).

These stories remind us that surrender isn't about understanding everything; it's about trusting the One who does.

THE TRANSFORMATIVE POWER OF SURRENDER

Surrendering to God opens the door for transformation. Romans 12:2 (NIV) reminds us: *"Do not conform to the pattern of this world, but be transformed by the renewing of your mind. Then you will be able to test and approve what God's will is—His good, pleasing, and perfect will."* When we release our need for control and trust in His plan, God renews our minds and strengthens our faith.

Neuroscientist Dr. Andrew Newberg notes in his book *How God Changes Your Brain* that prayer and meditation have profound effects on emotional health and resilience.

By focusing on God's presence, we activate neural pathways that foster peace, reduce anxiety, and enhance our sense of purpose. This scientific insight aligns with the spiritual truth that surrender leads to renewal and transformation.

A DAILY PRACTICE

Surrender is not a one-time event—it's a daily choice. Each morning, we have the opportunity to say, *"Lord, I trust You with today."* This act of surrender realigns our hearts with His will and invites His peace into our circumstances. Breath prayer is one practical way to cultivate surrender. As you inhale, silently say, *"God, I trust You,"* and as you exhale, *"I let go of all my fears."* This simple practice calms the mind and reinforces faith in God's promises.

REFLECTION QUESTIONS

As you reflect on this chapter, consider the areas of your life where you may be holding on too tightly.

What would it look like to release those fears and trust God with the outcome?

Where do you sense God calling you to release control and trust Him fully?

REFLECTION VERSE

Take a moment to open your Bible and look up the verse provided below. Read it slowly and prayerfully, letting God speak to your heart through His Word. Once you've read it, take time to reflect on its meaning. Write down how it applies to your journey, what it teaches you about

God, or how it encourages your faith. Let this be an opportunity to deepen your connection with Him through His Word.

Verse: *Romans 6:13*

Reflection: Reflect on what it means to fully offer yourself to God. How can surrendering to Him open the door for His righteousness to shine through you?

JOURNAL PROMPT/PRAYER

Journal Prompt:

Write about a situation in your life where you've been struggling to surrender control. What might change if you chose to trust God fully?

Prayer: Lord, I release my fears, doubts, and need for control into Your hands. Teach me to trust in Your perfect will and to find peace in surrendering to You. Renew my mind and transform my heart, so that I may walk in faith and confidence in Your promises. Amen.

CHAPTER THREE

EMBRACING A GROWTH MINDSET

THE STRUGGLE BETWEEN FIXED AND GROWTH MINDSETS

Life often feels like a series of challenges—seasons of pain, failure, and uncertainty that leave us questioning how to move forward. It's in these moments that our mindset becomes one of the most powerful tools for growth. How we view ourselves and our struggles shapes the way we respond and, ultimately, the way we grow. *Do we believe we're stuck where we are, or do we trust that transformation is possible?*

There are two primary mindsets: a fixed mindset and a growth mindset. A fixed mindset believes abilities and circumstances are unchangeable, that we're defined by our failures and limited by our past experiences. A growth mindset, on the other hand, believes in the possibility of change and development. It sees failures as opportunities to learn and trusts that God can use every moment to shape us into who He created us to be.

As Christians, we are called to embrace a growth mindset. This isn't about striving for perfection or worldly success but about believing in God's transformative power at work within us. It's a mindset that allows us to grow through every hardship, trusting that His purpose is greater than our present struggles.

THE DANGERS OF A FIXED MINDSET

A fixed mindset is like a self-imposed prison. It convinces us that our worth is determined by our mistakes, that our pain defines us, and that we will never be anything more. This mindset keeps us stuck, robbing us of hope and preventing us from experiencing the fullness of God's plan for our lives.

When we adopt a fixed mindset, challenges feel insurmountable. We shy away from new opportunities, fearing failure, and remain stuck in the belief that we're too broken to be made whole. The danger of this mindset is that it feeds the lie that God cannot use us in our brokenness or that we are unworthy of His transformative grace.

I know this feeling all too well. Throughout my marriage, I often had a fixed mindset, particularly during times when problems frequently arose and during our first separation. I found myself believing that my failures and pain defined me, trapping me in a cycle of hopelessness. In those moments, I felt utterly lost. However, during the time of reconciliation when the future was still uncertain, I reached a turning point. It was then that I surrendered to God, letting go of my desire to control outcomes and fully trusting in His plan.

THE POWER OF A GROWTH MINDSET

A growth mindset acknowledges that we may struggle, but we're not defined by those struggles. We have the power to grow, learn, and change, trusting that God is at work in us. Romans 8:28 (NIV) reminds us, *"And we know that in all things God works for the good of those who love Him, who have been called according to His purpose."* This scripture became my anchor as I learned to see setbacks as stepping stones.

True growth comes not only from a change in perspective but also from a heart fully surrendered to God's will.

Carol Dweck, in her book *Mindset: The New Psychology of Success*, highlights the transformative potential of a growth mindset. She describes how individuals with a growth mindset view challenges as opportunities to learn and improve. Similarly, as Christians, we can choose to see our struggles as opportunities for God's refining work in our lives. With each hardship, He shapes us to reflect His character and fulfill His purposes.

GROWTH THROUGH SURRENDER TO GOD

For Christians, a growth mindset is deeply tied to surrender. It's not about relying solely on our own efforts but about placing our struggles, plans, and limitations in God's hands. This act of surrender allows God to work through our challenges, turning our weaknesses into testimonies of His power.

The apostle Paul exemplifies this in 2 Corinthians 12:9 (NIV): *"But He said to me, 'My grace is sufficient for you, for My power is made perfect in weakness.' Therefore I will boast all the more gladly about my weaknesses, so that Christ's power may rest on me."* Paul didn't let his weaknesses define him; instead, he embraced them as opportunities for God's strength to shine.

Surrendering to God means acknowledging that we can't do it all on our own. With His grace, however, we can become who He created us to be. Each moment of surrender becomes a step closer to living out His plan for our lives.

PRACTICAL WAYS TO EMBRACE A GROWTH MINDSET

Adopting a growth mindset requires intentional effort and reliance on God's strength. Here are practical steps to help you move toward growth:

1. **Identify Limiting Beliefs**: Reflect on the thoughts that may be holding you back. Are there areas where you've told yourself, *"I can't change"* or *"This is just who I am"*? Bring these beliefs to God in prayer and ask Him to reveal His truth.

2. **Focus on Progress, Not Perfection**: Growth is a journey, not a destination. Celebrate small victories and trust that God is working in you, even when progress feels slow.

3. **Surround Yourself with Encouragement**: Seek out community, mentors, and resources that inspire growth. Proverbs 27:17 (NIV) reminds us:

"As iron sharpens iron, so one person sharpens another."

4. **Meditate on Scripture**: Fill your mind with God's promises and truths. Passages like Philippians 4:13 (NIV), *"I can do all this through Him who gives me strength"*, reinforce the belief that with God's help, growth is possible.

5. **Embrace Challenges**: Instead of avoiding difficulties, see them as opportunities to grow. When I faced a season of uncertainty during my divorce, I initially feared every challenge. But I began to see each trial as an opportunity for God to refine me and draw me closer to Him. James 1:2-4 (NIV) encourages us: *"Consider it pure joy, my brothers and sisters, whenever you face trials of many kinds, because you know that the testing of your faith produces perseverance. Let perseverance finish its work so that you may be mature and complete, not lacking anything."*

REFLECTION QUESTIONS

As you reflect on this chapter, ask yourself:

Are there areas of my life where I've adopted a fixed mindset?

How can I shift my perspective to embrace growth and transformation?

What steps can I take to align my thoughts with God's truth?

REFLECTION VERSE

Take a moment to open your Bible and look up the verse provided below. Read it slowly and prayerfully, letting God speak to your heart through His Word. Once you've read it, take time to reflect on its meaning. Write down how it applies to your journey, what it teaches you about God, or how it encourages your faith. Let this be an opportunity to deepen your connection with Him through His Word.

Verse: *2 Timothy 1:7*

Reflection: Meditate on this verse and think about how God's Spirit equips you to overcome fear and grow. What step of growth is God calling you to take today?

JOURNAL PROMPT/PRAYER

Journal Prompt: Write about a time when you overcame a challenge or limitation through effort and faith. How did that experience shape your understanding of God's power to transform?

Prayer: Lord, thank You for creating me with the capacity to grow and change. Help me to let go of limiting beliefs and embrace the truth of Your Word. Transform my heart and mind, and give me the courage to step into the plans You have for me. Amen.

CHAPTER FOUR

BUILDING CONSISTENT HABITS

THE JOURNEY OF TRANSFORMATION

Healing often feels like a race against time. I longed for instant change—to feel whole and restored all at once. But through my journey, I realized that transformation is not a single moment of breakthrough; it is a process. It unfolds slowly, through small, faithful steps taken every day.

At first, I didn't always see the fruits of my efforts. Some days felt heavy with doubt, and the routines I committed to seemed mundane. But I learned that the power of transformation lies in showing up consistently, even when results feel invisible. Every moment spent in prayer, every devotional read, and every act of surrender was building something within me, brick by brick.

Transformation isn't fueled by our ability alone; it's an act of faith. Each time I stayed consistent, even when I didn't feel like it, I leaned into God's promises. Over time, I began to see the fruits of my faithfulness—not only in my circumstances but in the deepening of my trust in Him.

THE ROLE OF DISCIPLINE

Discipline became the cornerstone of my transformation. It was the bridge between where I was and where I wanted to be. But discipline was far from easy. There were mornings when getting out of bed to pray felt impossible and days when the effort of surrender seemed futile. Yet, I chose to press on, trusting that my small acts of obedience were part of God's greater plan.

I remember one specific morning when everything felt heavy. The thought of opening my Bible seemed overwhelming, but I forced myself to sit down and read just one verse. That single act sparked a small but steady light in my spirit, reminding me that consistency, even in the smallest efforts, was building something eternal. Discipline taught me that consistency is not about perfection—it's about persistence.

On the days when doubt crept in, I found encouragement in wisdom shared by others. James Clear, author of *Atomic Habits*, emphasizes the importance of resilience when he writes, "Missing once is an accident; missing twice is the start of a new habit." This principle became a quiet reminder to reset and continue. Each time I returned to my routine, I felt stronger in my journey. I was becoming transformed with resilience and perseverance.

Each moment of faithfulness became a declaration that I believed in God's work within me. The habits I cultivated, no matter how small, aligned me with His will and moved me closer to the person He was shaping me to become.

BIBLICAL ENCOURAGEMENT FOR DISCIPLINE

The Bible offers numerous examples of the importance of discipline and consistency. Daniel's life is a powerful illustration of this principle. Despite living in a foreign land with challenges to his faith, Daniel maintained his habit of praying three times a day (Daniel 6:10). His consistent devotion to God prepared him to face trials with courage and faith.

Paul also emphasizes the importance of perseverance and discipline in 1 Timothy 4:7-8 (NIV): ***"Train yourself to be godly. For physical training is of some value, but godliness has value for all things, holding promise for both the present life and the life to come."*** This analogy reminds us that spiritual discipline strengthens our faith and prepares us for the life God has called us to live.

Discipline is not about rigid rules but about creating space for God to work in our lives. Consistency in our habits allows us to grow closer to Him and equips us to fulfill His purpose.

EMBRACING DELAYED GRATIFICATION

Living in a world that celebrates instant gratification, I often struggled with waiting. I wanted to see results now—to feel the rewards of my efforts without delay. But I learned that lasting change is born from patience. True transformation doesn't come quickly; it comes through faith in God's perfect timing.

The allure of quick fixes often tempted me to give up. But I began to see the beauty in delayed gratification. Galatians 6:9 (NIV) became a lifeline for me: ***"Let us not become weary in doing good, for at the proper time we will reap a harvest if we do not give up."*** The waiting wasn't wasted. It became a sacred space where God was at work, refining my heart and deepening my trust in Him. By embracing patience, I found peace in the process and discovered the joy of trusting His timing.

From a psychological perspective, the ability to delay gratification is linked to higher emotional intelligence and resilience. Carol Dweck, in her book *Mindset: The New Psychology of Success*, shares an example of how individuals who believe in their capacity for growth are more likely to persevere through challenges. Seeing struggles as opportunities to grow fosters both patience and resilience. Similarly, as Christians, when we resist the urge to seek quick fixes and instead trust in God's timing, we align ourselves with His greater plan.

The story of Joseph beautifully illustrates this principle. Sold into slavery and later imprisoned, Joseph endured years of hardship before seeing God's promise fulfilled. His faith and perseverance allowed him to rise to a position of influence and save many lives. Genesis 50:20 (NIV) reflects his trust in God's timing: *"You intended to harm me, but God intended it for good to accomplish what is now being done, the saving of many lives."*

Embracing delayed gratification also teaches us to rely on God's strength rather than our own. Isaiah 40:31 (NIV) assures us: *"But those who hope in the Lord will renew their strength. They will soar on wings like eagles; they will run and not grow weary, they will walk and not be faint."* By trusting in His timing, we cultivate patience, faith, and resilience.

SMALL HABITS, BIG IMPACT

When I began this journey, I believed that transformation required bold, dramatic changes. Over time, I learned that it's the small, consistent habits that hold the most power. The moments of prayer, quiet reflection, and surrender to God's will may have seemed insignificant at the time, but they were pivotal.

Each small act of faith, when repeated daily, created space for God to work. These habits compounded over time, leading to steady growth in my faith and alignment with His purpose. What seemed like small efforts were actually life-changing.

Once I began to embrace God's timing, I discovered how small, consistent actions could create lasting change. James Clear, in his book *Atomic Habits*, emphasizes that the cumulative effect of small, consistent changes over time creates lasting impact. This principle aligns with biblical teaching, as seen in Matthew 17:20 (NIV): **"Truly I tell you, if you have faith as small as a mustard seed, you can say to this mountain, 'Move from here to**

there,' and it will move. Nothing will be impossible for you." This verse reminds us that even small, consistent acts of faith have the power to create profound changes, as God honors our trust in Him.

Consider David, who faithfully tended his father's sheep before becoming king. His diligence in small tasks prepared him for the greater calling God had for his life. Similarly, Jesus Himself modeled the importance of consistent, small actions, often withdrawing to pray and seek the Father's will (Luke 5:16).

Practical examples of small habits include setting aside five minutes each morning to pray, memorizing one Bible verse a week, or writing down three things you're grateful for each day. These seemingly small actions can deepen your relationship with God and transform your perspective over time.

REFLECTION QUESTIONS

As you reflect on this chapter, consider the following questions:

What small habits can I begin today to align my life more closely with God's will?

How can I practice patience and embrace delayed gratification in my spiritual and personal growth?

REFLECTION VERSE

Take a moment to open your Bible and look up the verse provided below. Read it slowly and prayerfully, letting God speak to your heart through His Word. Once you've read it, take time to reflect on its meaning. Write down how it applies to your journey, what it teaches you about

God, or how it encourages your faith. Let this be an opportunity to deepen your connection with Him through His Word.

Verse: *Galatians 6:9*

Reflection: Think about an area where you need perseverance. How does this verse encourage you to remain faithful in small, consistent habits?

JOURNAL PROMPT/PRAYER

Journal Prompt: Write about a time when you practiced delayed gratification and experienced God's faithfulness. How did that experience shape your understanding of His timing and provision?

Prayer: Lord, thank You for the gift of discipline and the promise of transformation. Help me to build consistent habits that honor You and to embrace patience as I trust in Your timing. Strengthen my faith and guide me in small, daily steps toward the life You have called me to live. Amen

CHAPTER FIVE

THE POWER OF VISUALIZATION

THE BATTLE OF THE MIND

During one of the darkest seasons of my life, especially in the final year of my marriage, my mind became a battleground. Each day was filled with thoughts of pain, failure, and the overwhelming weight of uncertainty. My marriage had become a source of deep emotional struggle, and the toll it took on me physically and mentally was immense. I was trapped in a cycle of negative thoughts. The hurt from the past weighed on me, while the uncertainty of my future loomed large. Yet, even in this struggle, I realized something profound: I had the power to change how I thought.

I could choose to focus on my pain, or I could shift my focus toward something greater—something that reflected God's promises for me. The change didn't come overnight, but gradually, I realized my thoughts didn't have to define my future. Proverbs 23:7 (NIV) reminds us, *"For as he thinks in his heart, so is he."* This verse became a conviction for me: I had to be intentional about the thoughts I entertained. No longer could I allow the negative narratives from my past to dictate my life. Instead, I became intentional about what I allowed into my mind and thoughts. By focusing on truths rooted in God's Word, I created a mental space for hope, healing, and growth.

THE POWER OF SECLUSION AND INTENTIONAL WORDS

In the midst of my pain, I sought solitude. I intentionally stepped away from distractions and spent time in reflection, prayer, and silence. This period of seclusion allowed me to process my emotions and refocus my mind on God's promises. During this time, I guarded my heart and my words more than ever before. What I spoke to others, and especially what I said to myself, mattered greatly.

This intentional seclusion became the foundation for my practice of visualization. In those quiet moments, I found the clarity and peace needed to shift my focus from pain to God's promises.

I realized that retelling my pain repeatedly was not helping me heal. It wasn't beneficial; it only kept me trapped in the same cycle of hurt. The more I spoke about my pain, the more it seemed to control me. So, I made a choice. I stopped retelling the story of my hurt and began focusing on the victory that God was bringing about in my life. Philippians 4:8 (NIV) became my guide: *"Finally, brothers and sisters, whatever is true, whatever is noble, whatever is right, whatever is pure, whatever is lovely, whatever is admirable—if anything is excellent or praiseworthy—think about such things."*

By focusing on what was good, I shifted my narrative from one of pain to one of gratitude and hope. I began speaking life over myself, declaring truths that aligned with God's Word and His promises for my future.

VISUALIZATION: FOCUSING ON GRATITUDE, FORGIVENESS, AND AFFIRMATIONS

Visualization became a powerful tool in my healing process. I remember standing on the bridge during one of my walks, visualizing God's light surrounding me. In that moment, I imagined His peace washing away the fear and uncertainty that had consumed me. This practice of visualizing His promises deepened my gratitude and reminded me of His faithfulness.

Visualization also played a key role in my journey toward forgiveness. There were people who had caused me deep pain, and forgiveness didn't come easily. But through visualization, I focused on letting go of resentment. I would picture their faces and consciously release the weight of bitterness. Each time I visualized this, I felt a little freer. Forgiveness became less about the other person and more about the freedom it brought to my heart.

Additionally, I used affirmations to speak life over myself. I declared truths such as, *"I am loved," "I am chosen," and "I am equipped for the purpose God has for me."* These affirmations weren't just words; they were declarations of faith that helped me see myself as God sees me. Romans 12:2 (NIV) reminds us, **"Do not conform to the pattern of this world, but be transformed by the renewing of your mind."** Speaking these truths aloud helped renew my mind and align my heart with God's vision for my life.

SPEAKING LIFE: THE IMPACT OF WORDS

Words are not merely tools for communication; they are instruments that shape our subconscious beliefs and influence our actions. When we speak words of life, we reinforce patterns in our brain that align with hope, faith, and positivity. Conversely, negative words can entrench harmful thought patterns, making it harder to break free from cycles of doubt and fear.

From a psychological standpoint, this phenomenon is supported by the concept of neuroplasticity—the brain's ability to reorganize itself by forming new neural connections. Dr. Norman Doidge, author of *The Brain That Changes Itself*, highlights that our repeated thoughts and words physically alter the brain's structure. Speaking positive, intentional words grounded in truth strengthens neural pathways associated with faith and resilience. This aligns beautifully with Proverbs 18:21 (NIV), which tells us: **"The tongue has the power of life and death, and those who love it will eat its fruit."**

When we choose to declare God's promises over our lives, our words not only shift our mindset but also influence our actions. For example, saying affirmations like, *"I am loved," "God is with me,"* or **"I can do all things through Christ who strengthens me"** (Philippians 4:13, NIV) can help us approach challenges with renewed confidence and trust in God's plan. These words reinforce our faith, aligning our subconscious beliefs with the truth of God's Word.

BIBLICAL VISUALIZATION: A FOUNDATION OF FAITH

The Bible is rich with examples of visualization grounded in faith. Abraham, for instance, was called to visualize the fulfillment of God's promise. In Genesis 15:5 (NIV), God said to him: *"Look up at the sky and count the stars—if indeed you can count them."* This act of looking upward was a tangible reminder of the countless descendants God promised him. Abraham's faith was strengthened as he visualized God's plan, even before it came to pass.

Similarly, in Joshua 6, God instructed the Israelites to march around the walls of Jericho for seven days. Though the walls seemed impenetrable, they obeyed, visualizing the victory God promised. Their act of faith was rewarded when the walls fell.

Visualization in the Christian context is not about controlling outcomes but about aligning our hearts with God's vision for our lives. Hebrews 11:1 (NIV) defines faith as *"confidence in what we hope for and assurance about what we do not see."* By visualizing God's promises, we exercise this faith, trusting that He is faithful to fulfill His Word.

Practical Steps for Christian Visualization

1. **Anchor Your Vision in Scripture**: Begin by identifying promises in God's Word that align with your prayers and desires. Meditate on these verses, allowing them to shape your perspective.

2. **Create Time for Seclusion**: Set aside moments of quiet to focus on God's presence. Use this time to pray, journal, or reflect on the vision He has given you.

3. **Speak God's Promises Aloud**: Declare His truth over your life, speaking verses and affirmations that reinforce your trust in His plan.

4. **Visualize with Gratitude**: Picture yourself living in the fulfillment of God's promises. Thank Him for what He has already done and for what He will do in His perfect timing.

5. **Surrender the Outcome**: Remember that visualization is an act of faith, not control. Trust that God's plans are far greater than anything you could imagine.

REFLECTION QUESTIONS

As you reflect on this chapter, ask yourself:

What areas of your life need alignment with God's vision and promises?

How can you use visualization as a tool to deepen your trust in Him?

Are there words you need to speak over your life to replace fear with faith?

REFLECTION VERSE

Take a moment to open your Bible and look up the verse provided below. Read it slowly and prayerfully, letting God speak to your heart through His Word. Once you've read it, take time to reflect on its meaning. Write down how it applies to your journey, what it teaches you about God, or how it encourages your faith. Let this be an opportunity to deepen your connection with Him through His Word.

Verse: *Habakkuk 2:2*

Reflection: Visualize God's promises for your life. Write them down, and reflect on how keeping these promises in view can strengthen your faith and guide your steps.

Journal Prompt/Prayer

Journal Prompt: Reflect on a time when you trusted God for a breakthrough. How did visualizing His promises strengthen your faith?

Prayer: Lord, thank You for the gift of imagination and the ability to visualize Your promises. Help me to see myself through Your eyes, to speak life over my circumstances, and to trust in Your perfect plan. Strengthen my faith and guide me as I walk in alignment with Your will. Amen.

CHAPTER SIX

THE POWER OF GRATITUDE

THE POWER OF GRATITUDE

As my journey unfolded, there were times when life felt like it was unraveling entirely, leaving me caught in a storm of overwhelming emotions and uncertainty. The pain of my past and the uncertainty of my future threatened to overshadow every part of my life. But in those moments, I realized something profound: gratitude was my lifeline. It became the anchor that helped me stay grounded when everything else felt out of control.

Gratitude wasn't about ignoring my pain or pretending everything was fine. It was about intentionally shifting my focus from what wasn't working to what God had already blessed me with. The Bible reminds us in

1 Thessalonians 5:18 (NIV), *"Give thanks in all circumstances; for this is God's will for you in Christ Jesus."* I began to embrace this as a challenge—an invitation to find reasons to be thankful, even when I didn't feel like it.

The more I focused on gratitude, the more I saw the goodness of God. His provision, His protection, and His presence were evident in every area of my life. Gratitude didn't erase my pain, but it allowed me to see that God's hand was still at work, even in the messiness of my circumstances.

SHIFTING FOCUS TO GOD'S BLESSINGS

Gratitude required a deliberate shift in perspective. The pain and uncertainty were loud, but I discovered that focusing intentionally on God's blessings could silence the noise. I began keeping a daily gratitude journal, writing down ten things I was thankful for each day. The blessings I listed weren't always monumental; they were often simple and personal—my children, the reassurance of good health, God's protective care, the gift of salvation, and the stability of my job. Each entry became a thread in the fabric of God's unwavering faithfulness, reminding me that His presence was constant in every detail of my life.

After writing my list, I spent a few quiet moments reflecting on those blessings. I visualized them, allowing myself to feel the joy and peace they brought. I called out each one in praise, thanking God for His provision. This practice became more than just a mental exercise—it became a heart-centered experience that opened my eyes to the many ways God was sustaining me.

Gratitude also became a tool for combating fear and doubt. When I felt overwhelmed by uncertainty, I reminded myself of all the ways God had been faithful in the past. This reflection gave me confidence that He would continue to guide and provide for me in the future. Gratitude shifted my focus from what I lacked to what I already had, and in doing so, it brought me peace and hope.

GRATITUDE AS WORSHIP

Gratitude is not just a tool for personal growth; it is an act of worship. Psalm 100:4 (NIV) invites us to, **"Enter His gates with thanksgiving and His courts with praise; give thanks to Him and praise His name."** Gratitude draws us into God's presence, reminding us of His sovereignty and faithfulness. As I practiced gratitude, I noticed how it didn't just change me—it began to affect those around me.

I remember a specific day when the weight of my circumstances felt unbearable. I sat by the window with my journal, unable to stop the tears. At first, the act of writing down blessings felt hollow. My pen hovered over the page, unsure of where to start. But I began with the smallest things: God's love for me, the sound of my children laughing in the other room, the warmth of the sun streaming through the glass. Slowly, the list grew, and with it, so did a sense of peace. By the time I finished, my tears had turned to praise. This exercise became a daily ritual, a way of entering His presence with thanksgiving no matter how difficult the day felt.

Gratitude also reframed how I approached worship. Instead of focusing on what I wanted God to do, I began to celebrate what He had already done. Reflecting on His past faithfulness strengthened my trust in His future provision. As Lamentations 3:22-23 (NIV) reminds us: ***"Because of the Lord's great love we are not consumed, for His compassions never fail. They are new every morning; great is Your faithfulness."***

THE RIPPLE EFFECT OF GRATITUDE

One of the most surprising lessons I learned about gratitude is its ripple effect. Gratitude doesn't just transform our own hearts; it influences the people around us. When we express thankfulness, we create an atmosphere of encouragement and positivity that inspires others.

I experienced this firsthand when I began thanking the people who supported me during my hardest moments. Whether it was a kind word from a friend, a prayer from someone who cared, or simply the presence of a loved one, expressing my gratitude deepened those relationships. It also shifted the dynamic in my home. Gratitude became contagious. When I expressed thankfulness, it inspired others to do the same.

Research by Dr. Martin Seligman, a pioneer in positive psychology, highlights how gratitude strengthens relationships. Expressing appreciation fosters connection and builds trust. In Philippians 1:3-5 (NIV), Paul writes: ***"I thank my God every time I remember you. In all my prayers for all of you, I always pray with joy because of your partnership in the gospel from the first day until now."*** Paul's gratitude for those who partnered with him in ministry reflects how thankfulness builds community and brings God's love into our relationships.

THE TRANSFORMATIVE POWER OF GRATITUDE

In the beginning, gratitude felt like a struggle. The weight of my pain and the challenges ahead often made it hard to see the blessings in my life. But as I continued to practice gratitude, something began to change. I started to see God's hand in every part of my journey. What once felt impossible to overcome now seemed manageable because I was focusing on His power and faithfulness.

Gratitude became the bridge between my pain and the healing that was unfolding in my life. Each time I chose gratitude, I chose life. I chose to focus on what God had done rather than what I lacked. And in doing so, I found peace and hope that transcended my circumstances.

This practice of gratitude extended to how I interacted with others. I found myself expressing appreciation more often—thanking my children for their patience, acknowledging family and friends for their support, and even thanking God for lessons learned through difficult experiences. Gratitude shifted my focus outward, reminding me that God's blessings are not just for me but also for those around me.

GRATITUDE IN DAILY PRACTICE

Making gratitude a daily habit doesn't require grand gestures. It begins with small, intentional actions that shift our focus toward God's goodness. For me, it started with a simple journal. Each day, I wrote down ten things I was thankful for. At first, it felt mechanical. But over time, it became a sacred practice that connected me to God's presence.

Here are some practical ways to cultivate gratitude in your life:

1. **Start a Gratitude Journal**: Each day, write down ten things you are thankful for. They don't have to be big—a warm cup of coffee, a Scripture verse that spoke to you, or a smile from a stranger. Reflecting on these blessings trains your mind to notice God's goodness in the everyday.

2. **Express Gratitude to Others**: Take time to thank the people who have impacted your life. A heartfelt note, a quick text, or a simple "thank

you" can brighten someone's day and strengthen your connection.

3. **Incorporate Gratitude into Prayer**: Begin your prayers by thanking God for His faithfulness and blessings. Gratitude sets the tone for your conversations with Him, shifting your focus from requests to praise.

4. **Use Visual Reminders**: Place a note on your mirror, desk, or fridge with a reminder to be thankful. Scriptures like 1 Thessalonians 5:18 (NIV) can serve as inspiration: ***"Give thanks in all circumstances; for this is God's will for you in Christ Jesus."***

5. **Practice Gratitude During Challenges**: When difficulties arise, use your gratitude journal to reflect on your blessings or intentionally look for reasons to thank God in the moment. It could be for the strength to endure, the lessons you are learning, or the people He has placed in your life to support you.

REFLECTION QUESTIONS

Gratitude is a choice, and it's one that can transform every area of your life. As you reflect on this chapter, consider the following:

What are three specific things you are grateful for today?

How can you incorporate gratitude into your daily routine?

Is there someone you need to thank for their impact on your journey?

REFLECTION VERSE

Take a moment to open your Bible and look up the verse provided below. Read it slowly and prayerfully, letting God speak to your heart through His Word. Once you've read it, take time to reflect on its meaning. Write down how it applies to your journey, what it teaches you about God, or how it encourages your faith. Let this be an opportunity to deepen your connection with Him through His Word.

Verse: *Psalm 107:1*

Reflection: As you read this verse, think about specific ways God has shown His goodness in your life. How does gratitude transform your perspective?

JOURNAL PROMPT/PRAYER

Journal Prompt: Write about a time when gratitude shifted your perspective during a challenging season. How did focusing on God's blessings change your outlook?

Prayer: Lord, thank You for the countless blessings You have poured into my life. Help me to cultivate a heart of gratitude, even in the midst of trials. Teach me to see Your hand at work in all things and to give thanks with a joyful heart. Amen.

CHAPTER SEVEN

THE POWER OF FORGIVENESS

THE STRUGGLE TO FORGIVE

Forgiveness felt impossible at times. The pain of betrayal, the hurt of broken trust, and the weight of my past were often too heavy to bear. Yet, as I navigated this challenging journey, I began to see how forgiveness was not just about the past but about opening the door to healing and transformation. When I looked back on everything that had been done, I struggled to let go. The wounds from my marriage, the emotional abuse I had endured, and the people who had hurt me—all these things felt like chains binding my heart. I was trapped in the grip of anger, resentment, and unforgiveness, and I didn't know how to break free.

But as I moved further along my healing journey, I came to realize that forgiveness wasn't just a choice—it was a necessity. Forgiveness was not about excusing the wrongs done to me or pretending they didn't hurt. It was about releasing the hold that those offenses had on my heart, mind, and spirit. I had to understand that holding onto anger only kept me trapped in the past. It prevented me from moving forward and finding peace.

The Bible teaches us in Ephesians 4:31-32 (NIV): ***"Get rid of all bitterness, rage and anger, brawling and slander, along with every form of malice. Be kind and compassionate to one another, forgiving each other, just as in Christ God forgave you."*** I had to embrace this truth and let it guide my journey toward freedom.

GRATITUDE AS A PRELUDE TO FORGIVENESS

Before I could begin to forgive, I needed to align my heart with God's peace. Gratitude played a pivotal role in shifting my focus from pain to God's goodness. One evening, as I sat reflecting on my day, I realized how small blessings—like a kind word from a friend or the laughter of my children—helped me feel grounded in God's faithfulness. These moments reminded me that even amid my pain, His presence was constant, and this realization softened my heart, preparing me to forgive.

Each day, I practiced gratitude by reflecting on how God had been faithful throughout my journey. Whether it was through moments of peace, the joy my children brought, or the strength to face another day, these reflections helped shift my focus from the pain to the good God was still doing in my life. This wasn't just a list of blessings; it was a way to soften my heart and prepare me for the hard work of forgiveness.

As gratitude reshaped my perspective, I found the strength to begin releasing bitterness. Forgiveness wasn't about erasing the past but about trusting God to heal the wounds and fill my heart with His peace.

THE JOURNEY TO FORGIVENESS

Forgiveness has been one of the hardest, yet most transformative, steps in my journey of healing. The pain I carried from past hurts felt like a weight too heavy to bear, and at times, forgiving those who caused that pain seemed impossible. But as I wrestled with my emotions and sought God's guidance, I began to understand that forgiveness was not about excusing the actions of others or minimizing the hurt they caused. It was about finding freedom for myself—freedom from bitterness, resentment, and the chains of the past.

During one of the most challenging seasons of my life, I found myself clinging to anger as a form of self-protection. I thought that by holding onto my pain, I was somehow controlling the situation. But in reality, the anger and unforgiveness were only weighing me down, robbing me of peace and joy. I remember one night in prayer, pouring out my hurt to God. As I bowed in silence, I felt the full weight of my bitterness pressing down on me like a heavy stone. The anger and pain felt immovable, and for the first time, I admitted just how much they were controlling my life. Tears streamed down my face as I whispered, *"Lord, I can't carry this anymore."* In that moment, a flicker of peace entered my heart. It wasn't an immediate release, but I felt a shift—a willingness to begin the process of surrendering the hurt. Slowly, through His grace, I began to understand that forgiveness wasn't about excusing what had been done but about setting myself free. Slowly, through His grace, I began to truly understand that forgiveness was not about the other person; it was about setting myself free.

Matthew 6:14-15 (NIV) reminds us of the importance of forgiveness: ***"For if you forgive other people when they sin against you, your heavenly Father will also forgive you. But if you do not forgive others their sins, your Father will not forgive your sins."*** This verse struck a chord in my heart. Forgiveness wasn't just about obedience to God; it was about living in alignment with His grace and experiencing the fullness of His love.

THE VISUAL EXERCISE OF FORGIVENESS

As I sought God's guidance, I realized I needed a way to tangibly release the pain I was carrying. Once I grounded myself in gratitude, I began the challenging work of forgiveness. Forgiveness, I learned, is rarely a one-time act; it's a process that requires intentionality and patience. To help me, I practiced a simple visualization exercise that brought clarity and peace. I began to visualize God replacing my pain with His peace and strength, reminding me that I could rely on Him to carry what I could no longer bear. This repeated exercise not only eased the weight of my resentment but also deepened my awareness of God's constant presence and healing power.

WHAT FORGIVENESS DOES FOR YOUR MIND, HEART, AND BODY

Forgiveness is often described as a gift we give to ourselves, and science supports this truth. Studies have shown that holding onto anger and resentment can have serious consequences for both mental and physical health. When we forgive, we not only release the emotional burden but also invite healing into our minds, hearts, and bodies.

- **The Mind**: Forgiveness helps quiet the mental chatter of anger and bitterness that often accompanies unresolved pain. Research by Dr. Everett Worthington, a leading expert on forgiveness, shows that practicing forgiveness can reduce symptoms of anxiety, depression, and stress. By letting go of grudges, we free up mental space to focus on peace and joy, aligning our thoughts with God's promises rather than our pain.

- **The Heart**: Forgiveness softens the heart, creating space for love, compassion, and understanding. Ephesians 4:31-32 (NIV) encourages us to, ***"Get rid of all bitterness, rage and anger, brawling and slander, along with every form of malice. Be kind and compassionate to one another, forgiving each*** *other, just as in Christ God forgave you."* When we choose forgiveness, we reflect God's character, allowing His love to flow through us and restore our relationships.

- **The Body**: Unforgiveness has been linked to physical ailments such as high blood pressure, weakened immune systems, and chronic pain. According to Dr. Karen Swartz of Johns Hopkins Medicine, forgiveness can lower the risk of heart disease and improve overall physical health. Releasing the tension and stress associated with grudges allows our bodies to heal and thrive.

PRACTICAL STEPS TOWARD FORGIVENESS

Forgiveness is a process, and it often requires intentional effort. These steps are not just practical actions; they represent a way to align with God's heart and free ourselves from the burdens that weigh us down. Here are some steps to help you walk the path of forgiveness:

1. **Pray for God's Help**: Begin by asking God to soften your heart and give you the strength to forgive. Forgiveness is a supernatural act that often requires divine intervention.

2. **Acknowledge the Hurt**: It's important to recognize the pain caused by the offense. Pretending it didn't hurt only prolongs the healing process. Be honest with yourself and God about what you feel.

3. **Visualize Releasing the Pain**: Close your eyes and picture yourself placing the hurt, anger, and resentment into God's hands. Imagine Him taking it away and replacing it with His peace and love.

4. **Surrender the Pain to God**: Release the burden of anger and resentment by placing it in God's hands. Trust that He is the ultimate judge and will bring justice in His timing.

5. **Choose Forgiveness Daily**: Forgiveness is often not a one-time decision but a daily choice. Each

time the hurt resurfaces, reaffirm your decision to forgive and ask God for His continued strength.

REFLECTION QUESTIONS

Forgiveness is not just an act of obedience; it is a pathway to freedom and healing. As you reflect on this chapter, consider the following:

Is there someone you need to forgive? What is holding you back?

How has unforgiveness affected your mind, heart, and body?

What steps can you take today to begin the process of forgiveness?

REFLECTION VERSE

Take a moment to open your Bible and look up the verse provided below. Read it slowly and prayerfully, letting God speak to your heart through His Word. Once you've read it, take time to reflect on its meaning. Write down how it applies to your journey, what it teaches you about God, or how it encourages your faith. Let this be an opportunity to deepen your connection with Him through His Word.

Verse: *Micah 7:18*

Reflection: Reflect on the depth of God's forgiveness for you. How does His example inspire you to extend forgiveness to others?

JOURNAL PROMPT/PRAYER

Journal Prompt: Write about a time when you experienced the freedom of forgiveness. How did letting go of anger and resentment change your perspective and your relationship with God?

Prayer: Lord, thank You for the gift of forgiveness. Help me to forgive as You have forgiven me. Soften my heart and remove any bitterness or anger that hinders my relationship with You and others. Teach me to trust in Your justice and to walk in the freedom that forgiveness brings. Amen.

CHAPTER EIGHT

THE POWER OF PRAYER

BEGINNING WITH PRAYER

Prayer became a cornerstone of my healing journey—a sacred step after practicing gratitude and forgiveness. It was through prayer that I surrendered my burdens to God, sought His guidance, and found strength to move forward. Every morning, I began my day with a heart full of thanks, acknowledging God's blessings and asking for His wisdom. These moments of connection reminded me that I wasn't alone and that He was guiding me through every challenge.

Before focusing on my own needs, I intentionally prayed for others. Whether it was friends or family facing their own struggles, I found peace in lifting their burdens to

God. Philippians 2:4 (NIV) reminds us, *"Let each of you look not only to his own interests, but also to the interests of others."* By praying for others, I shifted my focus from my pain to their needs, and in doing so, I felt a sense of connection and purpose.

FOCUSING ON OTHERS

Praying for others opened my heart in unexpected ways. As I interceded for their struggles, I began to see my own pain in a new light. I realized that everyone carries burdens, and through prayer, I could empathize with their experiences. These prayers brought clarity and softened my perspective, helping me release the feelings of isolation I once held.

Each time I prayed for someone else, it reminded me of the interconnectedness of God's plan. We are called to lift one another up, to bear each other's burdens, and to extend grace. These moments of prayer became acts of service, aligning my heart with God's will and deepening my compassion.

THE IMPACT OF PRAYER ON HEALTH

Science and faith beautifully intersect when it comes to the benefits of prayer. Research has shown that prayer can have a profound impact on both mental and physical health. Studies conducted by institutions like Harvard Medical School and Duke University have found that regular prayer and meditation can reduce stress, lower blood pressure, and improve overall well-being.

When we pray, our bodies release calming chemicals like oxytocin, which can reduce the effects of stress hormones such as cortisol. This not only helps our mental health but also boosts our immune system. In layman's terms, prayer helps quiet the mind and calm the body, creating a sense of balance and peace. For me, these benefits became evident as I navigated seasons of uncertainty. The more I prayed, the more I felt grounded, capable of handling the challenges before me.

From a neuropsychological perspective, prayer can rewire the brain. Dr. Andrew Newberg, a leading neuroscientist, has studied the effects of prayer on the brain and found that it strengthens areas associated with compassion, empathy, and emotional regulation. This aligns perfectly with biblical teachings about prayer transforming our hearts and minds. Romans 12:2 (NIV) reminds us, *"Do not conform to the pattern of this world, but be transformed by the renewing of your mind."* Prayer is a tool God has given us to bring our thoughts into alignment with His will.

THE POWER OF SELF-PRAYER

After praying for others, I turned my focus inward—not selfishly, but humbly. I sought God's strength and wisdom for the next steps in my journey. I prayed for clarity, peace, and the courage to face each day's challenges. In 2 Corinthians 12:9 (NIV), Paul writes, *"But he said to me, 'My grace is sufficient for you, for my power is made perfect in weakness.' Therefore I will boast all the more gladly about my weaknesses, so that Christ's power may rest on me."* These words resonated deeply with me, reminding me that I didn't need to have all the answers—I only needed to lean on God's grace.

Self-prayer wasn't about perfection; it was about surrender. Each prayer became an opportunity to release my fears and trust in God's plan. As I laid my worries before Him, I found that His peace replaced my anxiety, and His strength carried me through moments when I felt weak. Once I began to trust God with my personal challenges, prayer became more than just a response to struggles—it became a constant conversation.

PRAYING BEYOND THE MOMENTS OF NEED

Prayer wasn't reserved for times of desperation. It became an ongoing conversation with God—a relationship built on trust, gratitude, and surrender. I learned to pray not only in moments of struggle but also in times of joy and gratitude. These prayers of praise reminded me of God's faithfulness and drew me closer to Him.

When prayer became a consistent part of my daily life, it transformed my perspective. I began to see challenges as opportunities for God's guidance and grace. Prayer helped me align my thoughts with His will, trust in His timing, and find peace even in the midst of uncertainty. It reminded me that I was never alone, and that His presence was constant, carrying me through every moment.

PRAYER AND RELATIONSHIPS

Prayer doesn't just impact our personal lives; it also transforms our relationships. When we pray for others, it shifts our focus from ourselves to those around us. It fosters empathy, compassion, and a sense of connection. James 5:16 (NIV) encourages us, *"Therefore confess your sins to each other and pray for each other so that you may be healed. The prayer of a righteous person is powerful and effective."*

Praying for those who hurt me was not easy, but it softened my heart and helped me see them through God's eyes. It allowed me to release resentment and replace it with compassion. This practice didn't just heal my heart; it also brought peace to strained relationships.

Prayer also strengthens bonds in healthy relationships. When we pray with and for our loved ones, it creates a sense of unity and shared purpose. In my family, praying together has become a source of encouragement and strength. It reminds us that we are not navigating life alone but are supported by each other and by God.

Practical Steps to Deepen Your Prayer Life

1. **Start Small**: If prayer feels overwhelming, begin with just a few minutes each day. Focus on honest conversations with God rather than trying to say the "right" words.

2. **Set a Routine**: Establish a consistent time and place for prayer. This could be in the morning, during a lunch break, or before bed.

3. **Incorporate Scripture**: Use God's Word as a guide in your prayers. Reflect on verses that speak to your heart and let them shape your conversation with Him.

4. **Keep a Prayer Journal**: Write down your prayers and the ways God answers them. This practice builds faith and reminds you of His faithfulness.

5. **Pray with Others**: Join a prayer group or partner with a friend. Praying together strengthens relationships and provides encouragement.

6. **Be Still**: Sometimes prayer isn't about speaking but about listening. Spend time in silence, allowing God to speak to your heart.

REFLECTION QUESTIONS

Prayer is a gift, a direct line to our Creator. As you reflect on this chapter, consider these questions:

How has prayer impacted your life?

What specific areas of your life could benefit from deeper prayer?

How can you incorporate prayer into your daily routine?

REFLECTION VERSE

Take a moment to open your Bible and look up the verse provided below. Read it slowly and prayerfully, letting God speak to your heart through His Word. Once you've read it, take time to reflect on its meaning. Write down how it applies to your journey, what it teaches you about God, or how it encourages your faith. Let this be an opportunity to deepen your connection with Him through His Word.

Verse: *Jeremiah 29:12*

Reflection: As you read this verse, meditate on the privilege of prayer. What does it mean to you that God listens when you pray?

JOURNAL PROMPT/PRAYER

Journal Prompt: Write about a time when prayer brought clarity, peace, or healing to a challenging situation. How did that experience shape your faith?

Prayer: Lord, thank You for the gift of prayer. Teach me to seek You in all things and to trust in Your guidance. Help me to make prayer a cornerstone of my life, transforming my heart and renewing my mind. May my prayers reflect Your will and bring glory to Your name. Amen.

CHAPTER NINE

THE POWER OF AFFIRMATIONS

THE FOUNDATION FOR AFFIRMATIONS

Affirmations became the final step in my daily routine, and by that time, I had already walked through the steps of gratitude, forgiveness, and prayer. Without those previous steps, I could not have fully embraced the power of affirmations. Gratitude had shifted my focus to God's goodness, forgiveness had released the pain of my past, and prayer had deepened my relationship with God. These practices cleared the way for me to speak truth over my life with confidence.

The affirmations I chose were rooted in God's Word but also reflected who I am in my family, my friendships, my work, my skills, and my purpose. These affirmations were not based on temporary feelings, the opinions of others, or mistakes from my past. Instead, they were grounded in the truths of who I am in Christ and the unique characteristics God had given me. I had to remind myself daily that I was more than my struggles, more than my pain, and more than the labels that had been placed on me. I am who God says I am.

AFFIRMATIONS AND HEALING FROM ABUSE

For anyone who has experienced abuse—emotional, verbal, or physical—affirmations become especially critical. Abuse distorts your sense of self-worth, often making you feel unworthy, invisible, or undeserving of love. It can cloud your understanding of who you are and your value. In my own journey, I struggled to see myself the way God sees me. The lies of unworthiness had taken root so deeply that I needed constant reminders of my true value.

Affirmations helped me see myself as God sees me—not through the lens of abuse or rejection, but through His love and grace. When you're constantly told you're not enough, it's easy to lose sight of your value. But when you begin to declare God's truth over your life, you start to reframe your worth. You realize that you are valuable, cherished, and worthy of love and respect—not because of anything you've done, but because of who God created you to be.

I remember a specific affirmation that became a lifeline for me during my healing: ***"I am fearfully and wonderfully made"*** (Psalm 139:14, NIV). Each time I spoke these words aloud, I felt a small piece of the weight of rejection lift. Slowly, as I repeated affirmations like this one, I began to believe them. I saw that my worth wasn't tied to the actions of others but to God's eternal truth about who I am. These affirmations not only reclaimed my sense of worth but also gave me the courage to set boundaries, expect kindness and respect, and align my life with God's vision for me.

Through these affirmations, I began to see that my worth was not determined by the hurtful words or actions of others. My value was grounded in Christ, and He had a good plan for me, despite what I had endured. These affirmations helped me not only reclaim my sense of worth but also raise my standards. I learned that I deserved to be treated with kindness, respect, and love. I no longer had to accept less than what God had intended for me. I could finally set healthy boundaries with others and stand up for myself.

AFFIRMATIONS, MENTAL HEALTH, AND PHYSICAL HEALTH

Mental health struggles, such as depression and anxiety, can cloud your perception of yourself. When battling mental health challenges, it can feel like your mind and body are at odds with the truth. Depression can make you feel hopeless and inadequate, while anxiety can leave you consumed by fear and self-doubt. In these moments, it's easy to get lost in negative thoughts or self-criticism. Affirmations, however, became my anchor, keeping me grounded in truth even when my emotions wanted to pull me into despair.

As affirmations helped heal my sense of self-worth, I began to notice how they also brought clarity and peace to my mind and body. In times of anxiety, I would speak affirmations that reminded me that I am capable of handling the day's challenges. When depression made me feel like I wasn't enough, I declared the truth that I am worthy of love, peace, and joy, regardless of how I felt in that moment. The more I repeated these affirmations, the more they became a lifeline. They kept me focused on the truth of who I am in Christ, even when everything around me felt uncertain or overwhelming.

Affirmations also have a profound impact on physical health. When we speak positive and life-giving words, it helps to reduce stress by calming our bodies and minds. This practice can lower levels of cortisol, the hormone associated with stress, and activate our body's natural relaxation system. Over time, this leads to benefits like better sleep, improved heart health, and a stronger immune system. When we choose to focus on affirmations rooted in God's truth, we remind ourselves of His peace and provision, which helps us stay grounded. The Bible captures this beautifully in Proverbs

17:22 (NIV): *"A cheerful heart is good medicine, but a crushed spirit dries up the bones."* This verse reminds us that what we speak and believe directly affects not only our emotional well-being but also our physical health.

THE ROLE OF THE CONSCIOUS AND SUBCONSCIOUS MIND

Affirmations work because they communicate directly with both the conscious and subconscious mind. The conscious mind often questions or rejects new ideas, especially when they challenge deeply held beliefs. However, the subconscious mind does not argue or analyze—it simply absorbs what it hears repeatedly. This is why consistent affirmations are so powerful. By repeating positive truths about ourselves, especially those rooted in God's promises, we can replace old, negative beliefs with new, empowering ones. Over time, these affirmations become ingrained in our subconscious, influencing our actions, thoughts, and attitudes. Carol Dweck, a psychologist and author of *Mindset: The New*

Psychology of Success, emphasizes that repeated affirmations can help shift our internal narratives, enabling lasting change. This process aligns with Romans 12:2 (NIV), which reminds us to be *"transformed by the renewing of your mind."*

SPEAKING TRUTH OVER MYSELF

In my affirmations, I would remind myself of these strengths. *I am resilient. I am compassionate. I am a loving mother, daughter, sister, and friend. I am equipped with wisdom, and I have the courage to face each day.* I would declare these truths over myself, and as I did, I gained energy, strength, and courage to face whatever the day held. Even when it felt difficult to believe them, I chose to speak these affirmations aloud. The more I repeated them, the more they began to shape my thoughts and my actions.

It wasn't always easy to speak these affirmations, especially when the weight of my past felt so heavy. But the more I affirmed who I was in Christ, the more I started to internalize these truths. They became a foundation that steadied me and gave me confidence in my identity. Speaking these affirmations not only reminded me of my God-given worth but also helped me walk in the fullness of the person God created me to be.

THE BIBLICAL IMPORTANCE OF AFFIRMATIONS

The words we speak have incredible power, a truth echoed throughout the Bible. Proverbs 18:21 (NIV) reminds us, *"The tongue has the power of life and death, and those who love it will eat its fruit."* Affirmations rooted in Scripture are not just about positive thinking; they are about aligning our hearts and minds with God's promises. Speaking His truth over our lives transforms us, renewing our minds as Romans 12:2 (NIV) urges: *"Do not conform to the pattern of this world, but be transformed by the renewing of your mind."*

The Bible is filled with affirmations of our identity and worth in Christ. Declarations such as *"I am fearfully and wonderfully made"* (Psalm 139:14, NIV) and *"I can do all this through Him who gives me strength"* (Philippians 4:13, NIV) remind us of who we are in God's eyes. When we speak these affirmations, we align our thoughts with His truth, allowing His Word to guide our actions and strengthen our faith.

STEPS TO PRACTICE AFFIRMATIONS WITH GOD

Affirmations are most effective when practiced consistently and with intentionality. Here are steps to help you incorporate affirmations into your daily routine:

1. **Ground Your Affirmations in Scripture as well as in your life**: Choose affirmations that reflect God's promises for your life. For example, declare, *"I am fearfully and wonderfully made"* (Psalm 139:14, NIV) or *"God's plans for me are for good"* (Jeremiah 29:11, NIV). Additionally, choose affirmations that speak truth over your role with others such as "I am loved and respected", "I am valued in my thoughts and

feelings", or "I am an amazing (mother, father, daughter, son, etc.)."

2. **Speak Them Aloud Daily**: Begin each day by speaking affirmations out loud. This activates both your mind and spirit, helping you internalize the truth.

3. **Use Visualization**: As you speak affirmations, imagine God's presence surrounding you. Visualize His love strengthening you and His promises being fulfilled in your life.

4. **Journal Your Affirmations**: Write down your affirmations in a journal each day. Reflect on how they align with your faith and how God is working through them.

5. **Repeat Them Throughout the Day**: Whenever doubts or fears arise, counter them with affirmations. This consistent practice helps renew your mind.

REFLECTION

Affirmations are powerful tools for transformation. They are not just words; they are declarations of truth that can shift our perspective, renew our minds, and empower us to live according to God's will. As I reflect on my own journey, I see how affirmations became a vital part of my healing and growth. They were a final step that helped me internalize the truths I had learned along the way—gratitude, forgiveness, and prayer. I had to remind myself daily of my worth in Christ, of my strengths, and of the unique purpose God had for me.

For those who have faced abuse or have struggled with feelings of worthlessness or mental health battles, affirmations are an essential step in rebuilding your sense of self. They help you break free from the lies and begin to see yourself the way God sees you: strong, valued, and full of potential. They keep you grounded in the truth of who you are in Christ, even when your emotions or struggles try to tell you otherwise.

REFLECTION VERSE

Take a moment to open your Bible and look up the verse provided below. Read it slowly and prayerfully, letting God speak to your heart through His Word. Once you've read it, take time to reflect on its meaning. Write down how it applies to your journey, what it teaches you about God, or how it encourages your faith. Let this be an opportunity to deepen your connection with Him through His Word.

Verse: *Joel 3:10b*

Reflection: Think about the affirmations you speak over yourself. How can declaring God's truth, even in weakness, shape your mindset and actions?

JOURNAL PROMPT/PRAYER

Journal Prompt: Write down three affirmations rooted in Scripture that reflect who you are in Christ. Reflect on how these affirmations can shift your mindset and bring you closer to God's truth.

Prayer: Lord, thank You for the power of words and the truth of Your promises. Help me to speak life over myself and align my thoughts with Your Word. Transform my mind and heart

CHAPTER TEN

EMBRACING THE FUTURE

THE BEAUTY OF NEW BEGINNINGS

As I reflect on my journey, I see how each step has prepared me to embrace the future with hope, faith, and confidence. The practices of gratitude, forgiveness, prayer, and affirmations were not just tools for healing—they became the foundation for living a life rooted in God's promises. Each practice built upon the other, transforming my perspective and allowing me to release the pain of the past. Now, I am ready to embrace the future that God has planned for me.

New beginnings can feel overwhelming, especially when you're stepping out of a season of brokenness. It's easy to carry doubts and fears into the next chapter of your life.

But I have learned that new beginnings are a gift—an opportunity to walk in alignment with God's purpose and trust His plan. Isaiah 43:18-19 (NIV) reminds us, *"Forget the former things; do not dwell on the past. See, I am doing a new thing! Now it springs up; do you not perceive it? I am making a way in the wilderness and streams in the wasteland."* This verse has been a cornerstone for me as I move forward, reminding me that God is always at work, even in the midst of uncertainty.

TRUSTING GOD'S TIMING

One of the hardest lessons I have learned is to trust God's timing. I've often wrestled with impatience, wanting things to happen on my schedule. But God's timing is perfect, and He knows exactly what we need and when we need it. Ecclesiastes 3:11 (NIV) tells us, *"He has made everything beautiful in its time. He has also set eternity in the human heart; yet no one can fathom what God has done from beginning to end."* This verse reminds me that while I may not always understand His plan, I can trust that it is good.

During my healing journey, there were moments when I questioned why certain doors weren't opening or why I was still waiting for answers. I remember one season when I felt stuck, unsure of why my prayers for clarity seemed unanswered. But in hindsight, I see how God used that season to refine me, teaching me patience and deepening my trust. When the door finally opened, it became clear that His timing was perfect and had prepared me for the opportunity ahead. Trusting His timing allowed me to release control and surrender my plans to Him. It also gave me the peace to move forward without fear, knowing that His plans are always better than mine.

SETTING GOD-CENTERED GOALS

As I embrace the future, I've learned the importance of setting goals that align with God's will. These goals are not about chasing success or worldly achievements; they are about pursuing a life that honors Him. Proverbs 16:3 (NIV) reminds us, *"Commit to the Lord whatever you do, and He will establish your plans."* When we invite

God into our plans, He directs our steps and aligns our desires with His purpose.

Setting God-centered goals begins with prayer and reflection. I ask myself questions like: *What has God placed on my heart? How can I use my gifts to serve Him and others? What steps can I take to grow in my faith?* These questions help me focus on what truly matters and avoid getting distracted by things that don't align with His will.

One practical way to set God-centered goals is to use a journal to reflect your spiritual and personal aspirations. Include Scripture verses, prayers, and specific goals that inspire you to stay rooted in your faith. Revisit these goals regularly, asking God for guidance and trusting Him to lead you.

WALKING IN FREEDOM

Embracing the future means walking in the freedom that Christ has given us. 2 Corinthians 3:17 (NIV) reminds us,

"Now the Lord is the Spirit, and where the Spirit of the Lord is, there is freedom." This freedom is not just about breaking free from the pain of the past; it's about stepping into the abundant life that God has promised.

As we set goals aligned with God's purpose, we can step into the freedom Christ has given us, unburdened by fear or doubt. For me, walking in freedom meant releasing the weight of shame, guilt, and fear that had held me back for so long. It meant choosing to believe that I am worthy of love, joy, and peace because of who I am in Christ. Freedom also meant letting go of the need to control every aspect of my life and trusting God to guide my steps. Each day, I remind myself that freedom is a gift, and it's up to me to walk in it with faith and gratitude.

EMBRACING CHANGE WITH COURAGE

Change can be intimidating, especially when it takes us out of our comfort zones. But change is often where growth happens. Joshua 1:9 (NIV) encourages us, *"Have I not commanded you? Be strong and courageous. Do*

not be afraid; do not be discouraged, for the Lord your God will be with you wherever you go." This verse reminds me that God's presence gives us the courage to face whatever lies ahead.

As I step into new opportunities and challenges, I hold onto the truth that God is with me. I don't have to face change alone because His strength sustains me. Embracing change with courage also means being willing to take risks, trust His leading, and stay open to the new things He is doing in my life. Each step of faith, no matter how small, brings me closer to the person He created me to be.

PRACTICAL STEPS TO EMBRACE THE FUTURE

1. **Reflect on God's Faithfulness**: Take time to look back on how God has guided and provided for you. Use these reflections as a reminder of His faithfulness as you move forward.

2. **Surrender Your Plans**: Release your own expectations and trust God to lead you. Pray for His guidance and wisdom as you step into new opportunities.

3. **Set Intentional Goals**: Create goals that align with God's will and purpose for your life. Write them down and ask Him to guide your steps.

4. **Stay Rooted in Scripture**: Let God's Word be your foundation as you embrace the future. Meditate on verses that inspire hope and trust in His plan.

5. **Celebrate Progress**: Acknowledge and celebrate the steps you've taken, no matter how small. Each step forward is a testament to God's work in your life.

REFLECTION QUESTIONS

As you reflect on this chapter, consider these questions:

What areas of your life do you need to surrender to God?

How can you embrace new beginnings with faith and courage?

What goals can you set that align with God's purpose for your life?

REFLECTION VERSE

Take a moment to open your Bible and look up the verse provided below. Read it slowly and prayerfully, letting God speak to your heart through His Word. Once you've read it, take time to reflect on its meaning. Write down how it applies to your journey, what it teaches you about God, or how it encourages your faith. Let this be an opportunity to deepen your connection with Him through His Word.

Verse: *Philippians 3:13-14*

Reflection: Reflect on what it means to leave the past behind and press into God's future for you. How does this verse encourage you to pursue His calling with hope and determination?

JOURNAL PROMPT/PRAYER

Journal Prompt: Reflect on a time when God's timing proved perfect, even if it wasn't what you expected. How did that experience shape your faith?

Prayer: Lord, thank You for the gift of new beginnings. Help me to embrace the future with courage, faith, and trust in Your perfect plan. Teach me to walk in freedom and to set goals that honor You. May my life be a reflection of Your love and faithfulness. Amen.

CHAPTER ELEVEN

CLOSING REFLECTION

A Journey of Transformation

As I bring this book to a close, I find myself reflecting on the incredible journey of transformation that God has led me through. From the depths of pain and brokenness to the heights of healing and renewal, each step has been guided by His faithfulness. Every chapter of this journey has been an opportunity to grow, to trust, and to discover the unshakable hope found in Him.

The practices we explored together—gratitude, forgiveness, prayer, affirmations, and trusting in God's timing—are not just tools for healing; they are ways to live a life that is deeply rooted in faith. They remind us that no matter what challenges we face, God's promises remain steadfast. Romans 8:28 (NIV) tells us, *"And we know that in all things God works for the good of those who love Him, who have been called according to His purpose."* This truth has carried me through every season, and it is my prayer that it carries you as well.

GRATITUDE FOR THE JOURNEY

Looking back, I am filled with gratitude for the journey God has taken me on. Gratitude has been a consistent theme throughout this book, and it is the practice that continues to shape my heart daily. I am thankful for the moments of clarity, the lessons learned through pain, and the joy of seeing God's hand at work in my life.

Gratitude has taught me to look for God's blessings even in the midst of trials. It has shown me that His goodness is present in every situation, no matter how difficult it may seem. I encourage you to continue practicing gratitude as you move forward, allowing it to anchor your heart in hope and faith.

A NEW PERSPECTIVE

This journey has given me a new perspective on life. It has taught me to see challenges as opportunities for growth, to trust in God's timing, and to embrace the beauty of new beginnings. I have learned that healing is not a destination but a process—one that requires patience, faith, and surrender.

As you continue on your own journey, I pray that you carry this perspective with you. Remember that every step, no matter how small, is part of God's greater plan for your life. Trust that He is working all things together for your good, and let that truth fill you with courage and peace.

ENCOURAGEMENT FOR THE ROAD AHEAD

As you move forward, know that you are not alone. God is with you, guiding your steps and strengthening you for the journey ahead. Joshua 1:9 (NIV) reminds us, *"Have I not commanded you? Be strong and courageous. Do*

not be afraid; do not be discouraged, for the Lord your God will be with you wherever you go."

I encourage you to continue building on the practices we have explored in this book. Make gratitude a daily habit, embrace forgiveness as a pathway to freedom, and let prayer and affirmations remind you of who you are in Christ. Trust in God's timing and walk boldly into the future He has prepared for you.

REFLECTION QUESTIONS

As you reflect on your journey and the lessons in this book, consider these questions:

How has God transformed your perspective through this journey?

CLOSING REFLECTION

What practices have been the most impactful for you, and how can you incorporate them into your daily life?

What steps can you take to continue trusting God and embracing His plan for your future?

REFLECTION VERSE

Take a moment to open your Bible and look up the verse provided below. Read it slowly and prayerfully, letting God speak to your heart through His Word. Once you've read it, take time to reflect on its meaning. Write down how it applies to your journey, what it teaches you about God, or how it encourages your faith. Let this be an opportunity to deepen your connection with Him through His Word.

Verse: *Hebrews 12:1-2*

Reflection: Open your Bible and read this verse carefully. Reflect on what it means to persevere in your faith journey and keep your focus on Jesus. Write down any hindrances you feel God is calling you to release so you can move forward with freedom and purpose. Take time with these verses, letting God speak to you through His Word. Write down your thoughts and insights, and let each reflection guide you deeper into His truth and love. This journey is yours, and God is walking with you every step of the way.

JOURNAL PROMPT/PRAYER

Journal Prompt:

What is one step you can take today to throw off a hindrance that is keeping you from fully embracing God's plan?

How can focusing on Jesus help you persevere?

Prayer: Lord, thank You for surrounding me with encouragement and the promise of Your presence. Help me to throw off everything that keeps me from running this race with joy and faith. Fix my eyes on You, Jesus, as the source of my hope and strength. Amen.

CHAPTER TWELVE

CELEBRATING GOD'S FAITHFULNESS

Reflecting on all that God is doing in my life fills me with awe for His transformative power. I often think back to specific moments in my journey when I felt like giving up, yet God faithfully reminded me of His presence each time. Those small nudges to keep going became turning points—moments that led to breakthroughs I never thought possible. Transformation doesn't always feel dramatic; it often looks like small, everyday decisions to trust God and keep moving forward.

I remember one instance when I felt defeated, but taking just one step—writing down a gratitude list—shifted my perspective entirely. This simple act brought clarity and renewed hope, reminding me that each small step toward

God can lead to life-changing transformation. Through this journey, I've come to see how God uses these moments to remind us of His presence and to strengthen our faith, even in the face of uncertainty.

THE PROCESS OF TRANSFORMATION

Transformation is not an overnight event. It's a process that unfolds as we take small, intentional steps toward God. Romans 12:2 (NIV) reminds us, *"Do not conform to the pattern of this world, but be transformed by the renewing of your mind. Then you will be able to test and approve what God's will is—his good, pleasing, and perfect will."* This verse became a guide for me as I sought to align my heart and mind with God's truth.

Post-divorce, life presents new challenges: being a single mom, maintaining a full-time job, managing my own home, and navigating financial responsibilities. Each day brings its own hurdles, but I take them one step at a time, trusting in God's grace and guidance. Spiritual practices, self-care, and community have become the foundation that keeps me grounded. With God's help, I've found that while life remains messy, it no longer feels overwhelming when I surrender it all to Him.

BUILDING A NEW FOUNDATION

These small, consistent disciplines became the framework of my new life, teaching me to trust God and find peace in His plan. I've learned that transformation is not about perfection but persistence. Each time I surrendered, I learned to forgive more deeply, extend grace more freely, and trust God more fully. As 2 Corinthians 5:17 (NIV) declares, *"Therefore, if anyone is in Christ, the new creation has come: The old has gone, the new is here!"*

God took someone who was full of anger, trauma, and resentment—someone who had built a fighter's defense personality—and transformed me into someone willing to surrender, forgive, extend grace, and trust Him. Even when my old self rises up from time to time, I'm reminded that transformation is a journey, not a destination.

This understanding has reshaped how I approach setbacks. On difficult days, I give myself grace while remembering I have two choices: stay in brokenness, feeling anxious, depressed, or angry—or reset, realign, and move forward. Through this transformation, I've learned that each small, intentional step brings me closer to becoming who God created me to be.

EMBRACING A LIFELONG JOURNEY

The journey of transformation continues. While challenges remain, I no longer walk this path alone. God has surrounded me with a network of support—family, friends, co-workers, and a counselor—each playing a vital role in my healing and growth. As I reflect on this journey, I am overwhelmed with gratitude. Sharing my story has allowed me to see God's hand at work not only in my own life but also in the lives of others. Each time I've opened up about my experiences, I've seen how God has used them to encourage, inspire, and strengthen both my faith and the faith of those around me.

Looking back, I see that God's transformation wasn't just about healing—it was about equipping me to live according to His will. Each trial and act of surrender became a building block for a life rooted in His promises. Transformation isn't easy, and there will be times when it feels like progress is slow, but don't give up. As you step into the days ahead, remember that God is always working in and through you. With every faithful step, trust that you're moving closer to becoming the person God created you to be.

LIVING IN THE OVERFLOW

Living a transformed life means living in the overflow of God's blessings. When your heart is full of gratitude, forgiveness, and truth, it overflows into every area of your life. Your relationships deepen, your perspective shifts, and your faith becomes unshakable. Transformation isn't just about personal change; it's about becoming a vessel through which God's love and grace flow to others.

Through these practices, you become a living testimony of God's faithfulness. Your life becomes a beacon of hope for those who are struggling, a reminder that healing and renewal are possible. As Matthew 5:16 (NIV) says, ***"In the same way, let your light shine before others, that they may see your good deeds and glorify your Father in heaven."***

CLOSING PRAYER

Lord, thank You for the journey You have taken me on and for the lessons You have taught me along the way. I am grateful for Your faithfulness, Your grace, and Your unending love. As I move forward, help me to carry the truths I have learned and to live a life that honors You. Strengthen my faith, guide my steps, and fill my heart with hope as I embrace the future You have planned for me. May my life be a reflection of Your glory and a testimony to Your goodness. Amen.

SCRIPTURE GUIDE

SCRIPTURES FOR TRANSFORMATION AND RENEWAL

God's Word is the foundation for renewal, transformation, and strength. These verses are organized to reflect the themes of this book—surrender, gratitude, forgiveness, affirmations, discipline, the goodness of God, strength, transformation, and love. Let these Scriptures guide your reflection, prayer, and daily habits as you walk in faith toward the life God has called you to.

SURRENDER

1. **Proverbs 3:5-6** — *"Trust in the Lord with all your heart and lean not on your own understanding; in all your ways submit to Him, and He will make your paths straight."*
   Insight: Trusting God means surrendering your plans to Him and believing He will guide your path.

2. **Romans 6:13** — *"Do not offer any part of yourself to sin as an instrument of wickedness, but rather offer yourselves to God as those who have been brought from death to life; and offer every part of yourself to Him as an instrument of righteousness."*
   Insight: Surrendering to God allows Him to use you for His purposes, turning brokenness into righteousness.

3. **Luke 22:42** — *"Father, if you are willing, take this cup from me; yet not my will, but yours be done."*

Insight: Jesus' surrender in the garden of Gethsemane shows the ultimate trust in God's plan, even in suffering.

4. **James 4:7** — *"Submit yourselves, then, to God. Resist the devil, and he will flee from you."*
Insight: Surrendering to God equips you with strength to overcome spiritual battles.

5. **1 Peter 5:7** — *"Cast all your anxiety on Him because He cares for you."*
Insight: Trusting God with your worries brings peace and reassurance of His care.

6. **Matthew 16:24** — *"Whoever wants to be my disciple must deny themselves and take up their cross and follow me."*
Insight: Surrendering to Christ involves self-denial and a commitment to follow Him fully.

7. **Psalm 37:5** — *"Commit your way to the Lord; trust in Him and He will do this."*

Insight: Surrender your plans to God, and He will work on your behalf.

8. **Jeremiah 29:11** — *"For I know the plans I have for you," declares the Lord, "plans to prosper you and not to harm you, plans to give you hope and a future."*
   Insight: God's plans for you are always good, giving hope even in uncertain times.

9. **Philippians 4:6** — *"Do not be anxious about anything, but in every situation, by prayer and petition, with thanksgiving, present your requests to God."*
   Insight: Trusting God involves letting go of anxiety and bringing your concerns to Him with gratitude.

10. **Isaiah 55:8-9** — *"For my thoughts are not your thoughts, neither are your ways my ways,"* declares the Lord. *"As the heavens are higher than the earth, so are my ways higher than your ways and my thoughts than your thoughts."*

Insight: God's plans are greater than our understanding; surrendering to His wisdom brings peace.

GRATITUDE

11. **1 Thessalonians 5:18** — *"Give thanks in all circumstances; for this is God's will for you in Christ Jesus."*
    Insight: Gratitude shifts your focus to God's blessings, even in challenging times.

12. **Psalm 107:1** — *"Give thanks to the Lord, for He is good; His love endures forever."*
    Insight: God's enduring love is a reason for constant gratitude.

13. **Colossians 3:17** — *"And whatever you do, whether in word or deed, do it all in the name of the Lord Jesus, giving thanks to God the Father through Him."*

Insight: Gratitude can be reflected in every action when it's done for God's glory.

14. **James 1:17** — *"Every good and perfect gift is from above, coming down from the Father of the heavenly lights, who does not change like shifting shadows."*
Insight: Recognize that every blessing comes from God, who remains constant and faithful.

15. **Philippians 4:8** — *"Finally, brothers and sisters, whatever is true, whatever is noble, whatever is right, whatever is pure, whatever is lovely, whatever is admirable—if anything is excellent or praiseworthy—think about such things."*
Insight: Gratitude starts with focusing your mind on God's goodness.

16. **Psalm 100:4** — *"Enter His gates with thanksgiving and His courts with praise; give thanks to Him and praise His name."*
Insight: Worship begins with a thankful heart.

17. **Hebrews 12:28** — *"Therefore, since we are receiving a kingdom that cannot be shaken, let us be thankful, and so worship God acceptably with reverence and awe."*
Insight: Gratitude flows from recognizing the unshakable gift of God's kingdom.

18. **Ephesians 5:20** — *"Always giving thanks to God the Father for everything, in the name of our Lord Jesus Christ."*
Insight: Gratitude becomes a way of life when you focus on God's blessings.

19. **Psalm 9:1** — *"I will give thanks to you, Lord, with all my heart; I will tell of all your wonderful deeds."*
Insight: A grateful heart overflows into sharing God's goodness with others.

20. **2 Corinthians 9:15** — *"Thanks be to God for His indescribable gift!"*
Insight: God's greatest gift—His Son—inspires unending gratitude.

FORGIVENESS

21. **Ephesians 4:31-32** — *"Get rid of all bitterness, rage and anger, brawling and slander, along with every form of malice. Be kind and compassionate to one another, forgiving each other, just as in Christ God forgave you."*
Insight: Forgiveness replaces bitterness and reflects the grace God has shown us.

22. **Matthew 6:14-15** — *"For if you forgive other people when they sin against you, your heavenly Father will also forgive you. But if you do not forgive others their sins, your Father will not forgive your sins."*
Insight: Forgiving others is essential to living in God's forgiveness.

23. **Micah 7:18** — *"Who is a God like you, who pardons sin and forgives the transgression of the remnant of His inheritance? You do not stay angry forever but delight to show mercy."*

Insight: God's mercy inspires us to forgive as He does.

24. **Luke 6:37** — *"Do not judge, and you will not be judged. Do not condemn, and you will not be condemned. Forgive, and you will be forgiven."*
    Insight: Forgiveness is a path to freedom from judgment and condemnation.

25. **Colossians 3:13** — *"Bear with each other and forgive one another if any of you has a grievance against someone. Forgive as the Lord forgave you."*
    Insight: Forgiving others reflects the forgiveness we've received from God.

26. **Psalm 103:12** — *"As far as the east is from the west, so far has He removed our transgressions from us."*
    Insight: God's forgiveness is complete, removing sin entirely from our lives.

27. **Isaiah 1:18** — *"Come now, let us settle the matter," says the Lord. "Though your sins are like scarlet, they shall be as white as snow; though they are red as crimson, they shall be like wool."*
Insight: God's forgiveness cleanses us completely and restores purity.

28. **Matthew 18:21-22** — *"Then Peter came to Jesus and asked, 'Lord, how many times shall I forgive my brother or sister who sins against me? Up to seven times?' Jesus answered, 'I tell you, not seven times, but seventy-seven times.'"*
Insight: Forgiveness is limitless, reflecting God's infinite mercy.

29. **1 John 1:9** — *"If we confess our sins, He is faithful and just and will forgive us our sins and purify us from all unrighteousness."*
Insight: Confession leads to forgiveness and cleansing through God's faithfulness.

30. **Romans 12:21** — *"Do not be overcome by evil, but overcome evil with good."*
    Insight: Forgiveness overcomes the power of evil with the goodness of God.

AFFIRMATIONS

31. **Joel 3:10b** — *"Let the weakling say, 'I am strong!'"*
    Insight: Speak God's strength over your weaknesses to find His power.

32. **Psalm 139:14** — *"I praise You because I am fearfully and wonderfully made; Your works are wonderful, I know that full well."*
    Insight: Affirm your worth as a unique and beloved creation of God.

33. **Philippians 4:13** — *"I can do all this through Him who gives me strength."*
    Insight: God provides the strength to overcome any challenge.

34. **2 Timothy 1:7** — *"For the Spirit God gave us does not make us timid, but gives us power, love and self-discipline."*
Insight: Affirm the power and courage God's Spirit gives to face life boldly.

35. **Romans 8:37** — *"No, in all these things we are more than conquerors through Him who loved us."*
Insight: Declare victory through God's love in every situation.

36. **Jeremiah 31:3** — *"The Lord appeared to us in the past, saying: 'I have loved you with an everlasting love; I have drawn you with unfailing kindness.'"*
Insight: Affirm God's eternal love and kindness in your life.

37. **Romans 8:1** — *"Therefore, there is now no condemnation for those who are in Christ Jesus."*

Insight: Declare freedom from guilt and shame through Christ.

38. **1 Peter 2:9** — *"But you are a chosen people, a royal priesthood, a holy nation, God's special possession, that you may declare the praises of Him who called you out of darkness into His wonderful light."*
Insight: Affirm your identity as chosen and loved by God.

39. **Ephesians 2:10** — *"For we are God's handiwork, created in Christ Jesus to do good works, which God prepared in advance for us to do."*
Insight: Speak God's purpose over your life as His masterpiece.

40. **2 Corinthians 5:17** — *"Therefore, if anyone is in Christ, the new creation has come: The old has gone, the new is here!"*
Insight: Affirm your transformation through Christ as a new creation.

DISCIPLINE

41. **Galatians 6:9** — *"Let us not become weary in doing good, for at the proper time we will reap a harvest if we do not give up."*
Insight: Consistent faithfulness and discipline lead to lasting rewards.

42. **Hebrews 12:11** — *"No discipline seems pleasant at the time, but painful. Later on, however, it produces a harvest of righteousness and peace for those who have been trained by it."*
Insight: Discipline may be hard, but it ultimately leads to growth and peace.

43. **1 Timothy 4:7-8** — *"Have nothing to do with godless myths and old wives' tales; rather, train yourself to be godly. For physical training is of some value, but godliness has value for all things, holding promise for both the present life and the life to come."*

Insight: Spiritual discipline has eternal value beyond worldly practices.

44. **Proverbs 12:1** — *"Whoever loves discipline loves knowledge, but whoever hates correction is stupid."*

    Insight: Embracing discipline helps you grow in wisdom and knowledge.

45. **1 Corinthians 9:25** — *"Everyone who competes in the games goes into strict training. They do it to get a crown that will not last, but we do it to get a crown that will last forever."*

    Insight: Spiritual discipline is compared to training for an eternal reward.

46. **Proverbs 25:28** — *"Like a city whose walls are broken through is a person who lacks self-control."*

    Insight: Self-discipline protects you like walls protect a city.

47. **2 Timothy 1:7** — *"For the Spirit God gave us does not make us timid, but gives us power, love and self-discipline."*
Insight: God equips you with the self-discipline to live a faithful life.

48. **Luke 16:10** — *"Whoever can be trusted with very little can also be trusted with much, and whoever is dishonest with very little will also be dishonest with much."*
Insight: Discipline in small things prepares you for greater responsibilities.

49. **Colossians 3:23** — *"Whatever you do, work at it with all your heart, as working for the Lord, not for human masters."*
Insight: Discipline in your work reflects your devotion to God.

50. **Psalm 119:105** — *"Your word is a lamp to my feet and a light for my path."*
Insight: Discipline in studying God's Word provides guidance for your life.

THE GOODNESS OF GOD

51. **Psalm 23:1** — *"The Lord is my shepherd; I lack nothing."*
Insight: God's goodness provides everything you need.

52. **Psalm 34:8** — *"Taste and see that the Lord is good; blessed is the one who takes refuge in Him."*
Insight: Experiencing God's goodness brings joy and peace.

53. **James 1:17** — *"Every good and perfect gift is from above, coming down from the Father of the heavenly lights, who does not change like shifting shadows."*
Insight: God's goodness is reflected in every blessing He provides.

54. **Lamentations 3:22-23** — *"Because of the Lord's great love we are not consumed, for His compassions never fail. They are new every*

morning; great is Your faithfulness."

Insight: God's goodness is constant and renewed every day.

55. **Nahum 1:7** — *"The Lord is good, a refuge in times of trouble. He cares for those who trust in Him."*

Insight: God's goodness is a source of comfort and safety.

56. **Psalm 145:9** — *"The Lord is good to all; He has compassion on all He has made."*

Insight: God's goodness extends to all His creation.

57. **Exodus 34:6** — *"And He passed in front of Moses, proclaiming, 'The Lord, the Lord, the compassionate and gracious God, slow to anger, abounding in love and faithfulness.'"*

Insight: God's goodness is rooted in His compassion and faithfulness.

58. **Romans 8:28** — *"And we know that in all things God works for the good of those who love Him, who have been called according to His purpose."*
Insight: God's goodness works even through challenges for your benefit.

59. **Isaiah 41:10** — *"So do not fear, for I am with you; do not be dismayed, for I am your God. I will strengthen you and help you; I will uphold you with My righteous right hand."*
Insight: God's goodness provides strength and support in difficult times.

60. **Matthew 7:11** — *"If you, then, though you are evil, know how to give good gifts to your children, how much more will your Father in heaven give good gifts to those who ask Him!"*
Insight: God's goodness exceeds human understanding.

STRENGTH

61. **Isaiah 40:31** — *"But those who hope in the Lord will renew their strength. They will soar on wings like eagles; they will run and not grow weary, they will walk and not be faint."*
Insight: Strength comes from trusting and hoping in the Lord.

62. **Psalm 46:1** — *"God is our refuge and strength, an ever-present help in trouble."*
Insight: God's strength is your refuge in challenging times.

63. **Philippians 4:13** — *"I can do all this through Him who gives me strength."*
Insight: God empowers you to face any challenge.

64. **2 Corinthians 12:9** — *"But He said to me, 'My grace is sufficient for you, for my power is made perfect in weakness.' Therefore I will boast all the more gladly about my weaknesses, so that*

Christ's power may rest on me."
Insight: God's strength is most evident in your weakness.

65. **Joshua 1:9** — *"Have I not commanded you? Be strong and courageous. Do not be afraid; do not be discouraged, for the Lord your God will be with you wherever you go."*
Insight: God's strength provides courage and confidence.

66. **Nehemiah 8:10** — *"Do not grieve, for the joy of the Lord is your strength."*
Insight: Joy in God brings strength and resilience.

67. **Ephesians 6:10** — *"Finally, be strong in the Lord and in His mighty power."*
Insight: God's strength equips you to face spiritual battles.

68. **Psalm 28:7** — *"The Lord is my strength and my shield; my heart trusts in Him, and He helps me.*

My heart leaps for joy, and with my song I praise Him."

Insight: Trusting in God's strength brings joy and protection.

69. **Habakkuk 3:19** — *"The Sovereign Lord is my strength; He makes my feet like the feet of a deer, He enables me to tread on the heights."*
Insight: God's strength enables you to navigate life's challenges with confidence.

70. **1 Chronicles 16:11** — *"Look to the Lord and His strength; seek His face always."*
Insight: Continually seeking God's strength sustains you.

TRANSFORMATION

71. **Romans 12:2** — *"Do not conform to the pattern of this world, but be transformed by the renewing of your mind. Then you will be able to test and approve what God's will is—His good,*

pleasing and perfect will."

Insight: Transformation begins with renewing your thoughts through God's truth.

72. **2 Corinthians 5:17** — *"Therefore, if anyone is in Christ, the new creation has come: The old has gone, the new is here!"*

    Insight: Through Christ, you are made new, leaving behind the past.

73. **Ezekiel 36:26** — *"I will give you a new heart and put a new spirit in you; I will remove from you your heart of stone and give you a heart of flesh."*

    Insight: God transforms you from the inside out, giving you a heart that aligns with Him.

74. **Galatians 2:20** — *"I have been crucified with Christ and I no longer live, but Christ lives in me. The life I now live in the body, I live by faith in the Son of God, who loved me and gave Himself for me."*

Insight: Transformation comes from living a life centered on Christ.

75. **Philippians 1:6** — *"Being confident of this, that He who began a good work in you will carry it on to completion until the day of Christ Jesus."*
Insight: God is faithful to continue transforming you until His work is complete.

THANK YOU FOR READING

Dear Reader,

This book was written with one purpose: to be a tool in your hands for transformation. I pray that through these pages, you've found encouragement, hope, and a deeper trust in God's plan for your life.

Healing and growth don't happen overnight, but each small step matters. On the hard days, give yourself grace. Keep moving forward, knowing that transformation isn't about perfection—it's about persistence.

If this book has encouraged you in any way, would you take a moment to leave a review? Your words could help someone else find hope and take their first step toward change.

Go to this URL to leave a review:

https://www.amazon.com/review/create-review?asin=B0DWLLLDJL

Or scan this QR code to go directly to the review page:

Thank you for being part of this journey. May God continue to restore, strengthen, and transform your heart every day.

With love and gratitude,
Tania Sandhu

Made in United States
Troutdale, OR
04/03/2025